Rainbow Rider

Rainbow Rider

Wannabe Biker 40 yrs. +
Takes Lessons

Linda Lou Jones

Psalm 45:1 "…my tongue is the pen of a ready writer."

Unless otherwise indicated all Scripture quotations are taken from the King James Version of the Bible.

Rainbow Rider
ISBN: 0980892937
ISBN: 9780980892932
Copyright 2018 by LINDA LOU JONES
All publishing rights belong exclusively to Rainbow Revelations
Publisher/Editor: Linda Lou Jones
Published by: Rainbow Revelations in Canada
Printed in the United States of America. All rights reserved under International Copyright Law. Contents and/or cover may not be reproduced in whole or in part in any form without the express written consent of the publisher.
Website: www.LindaLouJones.com
Other Books By Linda Lou Jones:
The Agonized Heart...No More – Abandon Abusers
Scalpel to Sword – Everyone Hurts Somewhere
Available from Amazon.com and other retailers
Soon to be Released:
Final Request – At Wit's End – Life Before The Cross
Praise The Lord – Life After The Cross
The Rent Is Paid – Monthly Miracles
Blog: https://www.rightlady.blogspot.com
Follow Me On Twitter:
https://www.twitter.com/rightlady7

Dedication

I Dedicate This Book To All:

-Male and Female Bikers
-Wannabe Bikers
-Re-fired Bikers
-Retired Bikers

We Have Something In Common:

Our heart skips a beat
When we hear
Varoom, Varoom!!

Let's Ride!

Contents

    Dedication ·v
    Preface · ix

1   Rainbow Rider · 1
2   The Fifth Encounter · · · · · · · · · · · · · · · · · 6
3   Stereotype Squished · · · · · · · · · · · · · · · · · ·20
4   Surrounded By A Rainbow · · · · · · · · · · · · · ·30
5   Knock, Knock, Knock · · · · · · · · · · · · · · · · · 34
6   Up, Up And Away ·40
7   One Potato, Two Potato, Bam! · · · · · · · · · · · ·51
8   Lookin' Good ·60
9   Eleventh Hour ·66
10 The 5th Amendment · · · · · · · · · · · · · · · · · · ·76
11 Second Chance ·86

Preface

If the vast range of emotions I experienced
During the birthing of this book
Do not trigger at least a grimace, a groan,
And even a huge burst of laughter and joy
Check your heart.
You may be dead!

☺

I lived it
Wrote it
It is a tool
To restore youth
Because
Laughter
Is
A Good Medicine

Even if it is
At myself.

Decades Later
Still Smiling

Want You
Smiling Too

1

Rainbow Rider

IF YOU HAVE unfulfilled desires in your heart, then read on and the following chapters will be sure to encourage you that the best is yet to come. Don't give up. Rather, you will have hope for your unfulfilled vision to be fulfilled, as mine was only yesterday. Mind you, it took almost thirty years, but it sure was worth waiting for. I'm convinced that it was the fulfillment of just part of a perfect plan for my life.

As you read on, imagine a new effectual door opening for you through which a deep desire of your heart will be fulfilled. Conditions will have to be met, but if you are willing to persevere you too shall be victorious. It is up to you whether you fail or succeed because it is you who must be motivated to do what is necessary for you to reach a particular goal. Failing to set a goal means failure to reach any goal. Setting a goal is the first step of a new beginning as you climb onward and upward regardless of circumstances. There may be some stumbling blocks that you will have an opportunity to turn into stepping stones, but it can be done if you so choose.

I trust you've got your mind in gear now and with an expectant heart a new spark will be ignited, resulting in a smile breaking forth as you grab hold of something beautiful. Something that is no longer a distant dream, but is about to become a dream fulfilled.

My dream or vision began when I was thirteen years old. One day as my brother and I sat in the back seat of the car my father was driving, enjoying a drive to the city of Toronto, Ontario, Canada, my ears were alerted to a strange noise. The source of the noise was a group of motorcycles about to fuel up. My eyes traveled from one bike to another...chrome shone from every direction. Then I viewed the drivers who sure looked tough to me with full beards, black leather jackets, blue jeans, chaps, leather boots, gloves, helmets, and women who looked equally as tough with lots of make-up and dyed hair that had obviously been back combed to the nth degree. Nevertheless, I was very impressed, intrigued, stimulated, fearful, even in awe at what I saw and heard. Surely this was a first.

My attention was then drawn to my mothers' words as she informed my father that she was sure she did not want to move to that section of the city. (We were looking for a house to buy and this was our first drive to this area...our last one too.) We never did move there, but I did take home with me seeds that were planted through what I saw and heard. Little did I know that those seeds would have such an impact on my life and for many, many years.

I had received a desire to ride on a motorcycle and be part of a group, yet my style and nature was very different from the females that I had just seen. To me they represented power, success, beauty, strength, confidence...all of which I believed I did not have. No wonder I wanted to be like them! Without even realizing it, they became idols to me at that young age, and even though I did not think about this group of bikers very often, seeds had been planted that would have quite an impact on my life.

Twenty-nine years passed by quickly, during which time I actually sat on a Harley-Davidson bike one time only…but that was simply frustrating because the bike was not running and I could not go for a ride. (The 8 x 10 photo of me sitting on it sure touched my heart though.) My second encounter with a bike was when I went for a very brief ride over a hill in a public park, but I feared falling off the back as we climbed, so the ride was short and not too sweet.

My third encounter was when I was a passenger on a dirt bike and rode quickly over a field which was very uneven…to say the least, and I must admit my heart was in my mouth more than once as we dodged apple trees throughout the field. The 8 x 10 photo of the two of us on that dirt bike clearly shows my concern.

My next encounter was as a passenger on a 500-c.c. dirt bike and for the first time I wore a helmet and gloves which somehow released a flow of adrenaline as the bike rolled forward. *But*, we rode on the most crooked gravel road I think I've ever been on, as we toured a cottage area surrounded by trees, the blackness of night except for the moon and stars, and from my viewpoint the potholes that were filled with rainwater looked equally as black. My legs ached from holding my feet off the ground because there were no pegs to rest them on and before this ride was over, I was beginning to wonder if biking was a good idea or not. Somehow it had failed to meet my expectations thus far. But…there was a fifth encounter coming that I did not know about.

2

The Fifth Encounter

This time a new door opened because first, I opened a door to someone. Only one year ago I stood face to face with a man who was looking for a place to room. His job transfer caused him to be separated from his family during the week until he could sell his home. An acquaintance of his asked me if I was interested in taking in a roomer, a roomer who is a Christian.

I had been saved for seven years at this time. My mother, who was a Christian and a widow; my Christian teenage daughter, and I, all lived together and we had considered taking in a roomer. It would be good to have a man around the house to deter thieves, etc. and we could use the money, so we agreed to meet with him. After a brief visit, we opened the door to him to room at our home.

Since I had been single again for ten years, it was nice to have a male viewpoint to listen to. Knowing there was a man in the home resulted in us women feeling safer. God was using the boarder to help us and visa versa. Since God promises that He will put the solitary in families I could see clearly how all of us were being favored. God had a plan.

Little did I know the surprise I was about to receive. I looked out the kitchen window and in drove our new roomer on a great big motorcycle.! I could hardly believe my eyes. It was so beautiful. Soon I learned that before his job transfer he was the president of a Christian motorcycle club. The more I heard the more I could hardly believe what I was hearing. He said he would give me a ride on the bike someday, and you can be sure I prayed that he would not forget.

I had some time to do some thinking before he took me on that ride and my heart was deeply moved when I pieced together part of God's plan for my life. You see, God knows the desires of my heart yet He protected me from the outlaw bikers...even before I got saved...when I was living in sin...God kept me from them and them from me. But now was the time for me to ride down that highway and I wanted to go so badly. Finally, the big evening arrived. I borrowed a helmet from a neighbor, leather jacket from my daughter, got my gloves and western boots and closed the door behind me.

As I walked across the front yard it was hard to keep my feet on the ground. This would be my first time ever to ride a street bike and the weather was perfect...at least I thought it was. The sun was shining and there were beautiful billowy white clouds in the blue sky.

After receiving directions from the driver as to where to put my feet and what to do as well as what not to do, I slowly and carefully got on the 1100 c.c. bike, said a quick prayer for traveling mercies and we were off. First, we fueled up, then we headed out of town on a good paved highway.

It was at that time I realized I had a big smile on my face and it just would not leave. I couldn't help smiling for the life of me, my heart was so happy I thought it would explode. Then I came back down to earth because the wind caught my sunglasses (or if you live in Texas, you say "sunshades") and the next thing I knew they were knocked to the right of my nose...even though I was wearing a helmet! Lesson number one, if your protective clothing is not a proper fit, don't expect to be properly protected. I had a decision to make. Would I ride with my head turned sideways in order to keep my sunglasses on in the cross wind; or would I look around and enjoy the rolling hills and green fields, trusting that there would not be a repeat performance. I chose to enjoy the view while frequently adjusting the glasses.

Often, I found myself gasping for air because it was so windy and for a time we had to drive through the crosswind. Mind you I didn't complain though. Those wheels just kept turning under me as we rode along and soon I could not feel the seat of the bike under me (relax, I didn't fall off, I just arose above the circumstances and was doing what Christians call "soaring in the spirit...soaring like an eagle!). If you've never done it, ask God to give you an experience such as I had, He is no respecter of persons.

The following lyrics are for a song I wrote after the bike ride that I had wanted to go on so badly, especially for the past ten years. Title of the song:

Never.... Never... Never!

Never, never, never, ever should there be
A motorcycle with just one
Rider
When two can have such fun!

How do I know?
'Cause I just went for a ride.
I couldn't wipe the smile off my face
'Cause of the joy I felt inside.

I waited ten years for that ride.
God knows…

RAINBOW RIDER

And I was thrilled
Right to my toes!

I soared like an eagle
Rollin' down that highway.
Never felt my feet or my seat,
On that bike.
I flew to the mountaintop that day!

We sang lots of songs, unto the Lord
In harmony
We sang to Jesus because
He set us *Free!*

Little did I know that this ride was just the beginning of many because that summer I rode over 1500 miles as a passenger (mostly local driving) and loved every minute of it. There was no fear, it was a big bike and very heavy so this helped me to feel more secure, but more importantly, I knew God had prepared the way for me to do this; so, I trusted Him to keep me alive while I was out there on the highways and so far, so good, praise God.

Also, I knew the Lord had given me an excellent driver so I never once worried about him popping wheelies, etc. I knew I was with a qualified experienced driver as well as a Christian gentleman so I just sat back and enjoyed the ride, as only a passenger can! (I might add that I became a passenger only after receiving permission from this man's wife and each time we went for a bike ride we were home before dark as per our agreement.) His wife drove her own bike and their children were bikers also.

Since my home is in Bowmanville, Ontario, and his home is in Kincardine, Ontario, we rode to his home on Friday night after work one time. It was a good four-hour drive by car, and since this was my first long bike ride, we stopped every hour for about five minutes to stretch our legs, and move around a bit. I was fine until the last twenty minutes. The sun had gone down and the dampness set in very quickly.

From my knees to my hips I felt like I had been in a cold river and the water was about to freeze. The aching was so deep in such a short time, until finally, much as I hated to give in, I asked the driver to stop. I dug out some legwarmers and pulled them up as far as they would go, but I knew I was in trouble. My right leg was so still I had to drag it off the bike and I felt like crying, but I was too cold to even do that. I prayed and we finally pulled into the driveway. The lights of that house sure looked inviting. I must confess I was pretty concerned about how I would ever ride from Kincardine to Niagara Falls, Ontario the following morning as had been planned.

Again, another lesson learned. If you are going to be doing some night driving, dress appropriately, leather pants are a must if you intend to keep warm, not to mention the protection they provide in case of a fall. If you are going swimming you don't wear a jogging suit, so when you ride a bike, dress for the occasion…for your own good. If for yourself…you care…proper clothing you'll wear! You can't afford *not* to!

God answered prayer and after a good night's sleep, I was just fine, thawed out, and roaring to go again! His wife and two boys went also and the adrenaline was flowing from all directions as we headed out.

International Christian Bikers Association is the name of the group of bikers I began to get to know as I attended certain functions they had planned throughout the summer months. Every Thursday the Peterborough, Ontario bikers had a bike run so I was happy to join them one evening. It was news to me that the President did not lead the group on the run; that was the Road Captain's job. Prior to leaving he advised the drivers of the intended route. They did their safety check then left for a tour for a few hours. The bikers rode in staggered formation, following fairly closely. We enjoyed the rolling hills and beautiful weather. I was especially touched by the way God had so gently led me into biking. He never pushes, He leads us lovingly, one step at a time.

After the bike run we met at a particular restaurant and it was great to fellowship together. For the unsaved readers, fellowship means visit, but that is really an understatement because when Christians, brothers and sisters in the Lord visit, there is a closeness and unity that the unsaved do not know of, because the Holy Spirit binds us together in love. It is a bond of love only God can give and this love is so strong it allows perfect strangers to be able to open up with each other and share freely. The masks are gone and there is a desire to release love from an open heart to others. In doing so, you receive the same because you reap what you sow. It's great and it has God's anointing upon it.

Another happy memory was when we met the bikers at a restaurant and enjoyed fellowshipping together. They do this once a month and it is food for the soul when Jesus is lifted up, not to mention the food we received for the body. It was a good witness to others too, because the average restaurant clientele does not expect bikers to bow their heads and say grace before a meal. Such a simple heartfelt prayer has been known to tug on more than one heartstring as God uses Christian bikers effectively.

My first get together with I.C.B.A. members from many areas was when I attended a pig roast in Gorrie, Ontario. When we drove to the farm where it was held, I marveled at how closely the bikes were parked. One slip and the whole line would have ricochet…or so it appeared.

As we entered the driveway, we were handed a little 3"x3" thin piece of plywood upon which the kickstand rested, rather than each kickstand leaving a footprint in the lawn. When I saw all of those bikes lined up I thought I was in heaven, they looked so beautiful. It was like being a step closer to heaven and I was sure excited, though I tried to be somewhat dignified.

This first gathering sure was different than any I had ever even dreamed of attending because the bikers sat on makeshift benches and sang choruses to the Lord in the evening for a while. Not only that, but they danced unto the Lord, and they were smiling, smiling, smiling!!! Sure, they compared bikers, talked about upcoming events, etc., but they uplifted Jesus Christ, knowing full well that it was Jesus who brought them together and had kept them safe thus far. My heart was full when I saw men with beards and lots of muscles lifting their arms up high as a sign of surrender to the Lord. The tough man is not the big strong man, rather, the "tough man" is the man with a "tender (full of Jesus) heart"!!!

I bought a T-shirt with the biker's crest on it, a key chain, and a beautiful leather belt that had the following words on it: **'Riding For The Son'.** *Now that is what I call a belt!* The front of the T-shirt said the same. (If you are not a Christian you may think it is crazy to wear something that is worded like this, but I can boldly tell you it is not crazy, it is a very rewarding thing to do because it is called letting your light shine. When you've got something as good as a personal relationship with Jesus Christ, then there is no hesitation in letting your light shine because you want others to receive the answer to all their problems too. Besides, if you haven't tried Jesus, don't knock him, or anyone who uplifts him because the Bible says, "Touch not my anointed." And if you think you can throw stones at God's anointed without any repercussions, you are mistaken. God is a just God and revenge is His so the Christians are on the winning side because God is on their side, and He *always* sees that justice is done when we lift to Him our problems and concerns. That's why I do not hesitate to share Jesus with others. I *know* that **Jesus…is the answer!**

Maybe you thought this book was strictly about motorcycles, and now you aren't too sure whether to read on or not. Well, my heart is talking directly to your heart, so why not read on because there is something very important I want to say to you…yes, you.

You are special to someone, and that someone is none other than God. He created you and He loves you just as you are. He has a perfect plan for your life and He wants to help you on a daily basis…if you will let Him. He understands how you feel, even better than you do. He loves you so much that He led you to read this book so He could talk to you. You wouldn't read the Bible, but that doesn't stop God from getting through to you. Nothing is too hard for Him and when He wants to talk to you He knows how to get through, so please...stop struggling and let God have control of your life. His ways really do satisfy. All I ask is that you keep reading and I pray that as I share some of the things I have experienced as a new biker, you will clearly see how God has given me a new life and fulfilled desires of my heart in better ways than I could have ever done. Now chin up, and read on, because I think you will really be surprised when you learn how the Lord moved me forward...to say the least!!!

Let's move on to the Niagara Falls' Son Rally that I attended last summer because there were some very unexpected events, much to my pleasure (at least most of them were). Suffice to say that when you are in a soul winning ministry you can be sure there will be some persecution, and I had my share of persecution...through Christians; but God enabled me to forgive many times, and to keep my eyes on the Lord.

In doing so, I also receive the victory; victory in Jesus! God is faithful to honor obedience. He is not like people who call themselves Christians, listen to gossip and evil reports, believe the reports, judge...

condemn...and reject the person talked about, then go their merry way praising the Lord. God is love and it is by our love that others will know that we are Christians. If the love is gone, where is Jesus? And if Jesus is not there, which highway are you traveling on, the holy highway that leads to heaven, or the highway that leads to hell...?

Jeepers, I thought this book was going to be for all bikers, saved and unsaved, as I shared personal experiences but what I didn't realize is that because Jesus loves bikers too, He is using this book to talk to you all (in Texas they say y'all), so some of these insertions are as much a surprise to me as they are to you. It may seem like I am getting off track, but what is happening is that some of you are getting *on track*! It is so great when God is in control because there are no limits with Him.

Speaking of control, it was an exciting moment when the bikers lined up their highly polished bikers and the line of about 160 bikes with a police escort headed for Niagara Falls, Canada. The adrenaline was flowing and I was about to learn a few things regarding the general public's opinion of bikers.

3

Stereotype Squished

Peoples' reactions reveal much. The tourists at Niagara Falls totally shocked me. I observed their glance in our direction as they heard the initial bikes arrive, then did a double take as they spotted more bikes. This was followed by yet a third look as they viewed a full line of bikers on the roadway for as far as they could see ahead and behind. Simultaneously, women quickly grabbed their children and clutched them to their bosom, while anxious husbands searched quickly for an end to this line-up.

They hastily arose to their feet, abandoning the blankets strewn with food as their picnic was interrupted. Sunbathers quickly stood to their feet while clutching towels in an effort to protect themselves. It seems they could expose their flesh to the sunshine and the public uninhibitedly, but before bikers, they felt intimidated. Their eyes reflected fear and question marks.

My heart filled with compassion for them when I saw their reactions. If they only knew, we were not here to hurt them, but to love them as we share Jesus with them. Nevertheless, I could not blame them because there was a time when I felt the same way... when I was only thirteen years old in Toronto and I recalled it like yesterday. This realization sparked me to do what I could in an effort to help the public learn that not all bikers are outlaw bikers. I decided it was time that old stereotype be squished and a new stereotype rise up like a beacon before the public eye as Jesus Christ shone more brightly than any chrome!

I learned another lesson in Niagara Falls that weekend when I did a "no-no" on the bike! We came to a full stop as the first bikes were gradually parked in a designated area. I felt the refreshing mist hit my face as we sat in the hot sun, directly in front of Niagara Falls. With my camera clutched tightly in my hand and my feet planted solidly on the foot pegs, I slowly and steadily raised myself up then my upper torso did a slow right turn while I took aim with the camera. One second and I did an about turn until I was facing directly forward and still raised up off the seat, when suddenly with more loudness than usually and with a voice of authority, I heard the driver say: *"I'm leaving now!"*

I can tell you I got in gear in a hurry as I sat down instantly and kept my mouth shut…believe it or not! It was at that moment I realized had I been the driver who was stopped, balancing the heavy bike…with a passenger on the back…I would certainly not appreciate any unnecessary activity on the back especially when I was at a full stop. Common sense could tell anyone that, so it was a good thing I did not get a blast right then and there, or worse still, be made to walk! So, if you drive with a passenger I suggest you inform your passenger prior to the ride that there are certain "no-no's."

The traffic cleared and when the bikes were parked I started to survey the situation. Some of the bikers were resting on the grass and listening to some gospel singers. Other bikers had decided to go for a walk to view Niagara Falls, while yet others were beginning to evangelize right there at the park. There were lots of people and it was great weather that weekend.

I had several tracts in my hand to give out. A tract is a little animated booklet that tells the true story of the President of I.C.B.A. (International Christian Bikers Association). It tells what his life was like prior to his salvation, and what it is like now that he has accepted Jesus Christ as his Savior and Lord of his life. Freedom Rider is the title and shows a sketch of a man on a motorcycle. God gives you the tools you need to do the job and these tracts were tools that He would use to spread the Good News.

As I looked at all those 160 bikes lined up with the sun shining on all the chrome, it crossed my mind that some people might think there was a funeral taking place. I recalled watching the news on television when a biker had died and the film crew televised the bikers as they were on route to the funeral. But this was no funeral, it was a resurrection that we were celebrating. The resurrection of none other than Jesus Christ! The following poem best describes what happened in the next moments of the summer.

LINDA LOU JONES

The Little Book

As I walked up the sloped entrance
To the park
Admiring the motorcycles
Parked alongside,
In the vine (John Chapter 15)
I did abide.
My hand held some little books
To give out.
I prayed, "Lord, show me who
To give these to,
Let there be no doubt."
About five steps later
I felt a gentle tug on my arm.
I turned and looked down
At a child's innocent face.
He said, "Um, how much
Do those little books cost?"
My heart filled with love
As I looked into his questioning eyes.
This eleven year old Chinese boy
Was hungry spiritually.
There was no disguise.

Somewhat hesitantly he asked me,
"Did someone die?"
Again, my heart was full
As I thought of Jesus and Calvary,
But this boy asked
Because he had just seen
160 motorcycles drive through
To the park...
We sat by the curb
As I shared a beautiful love story.
He then prayed with me,
The sinner's prayer.
To God be the glory.

Squeezing the little book "Freedom Rider"
He told me he had never been
To Sunday school.
We shook hands
Then I hugged him briefly,
A new pen pal.
God's love is a powerful tool.
It is our greatest warfare weapon.
What do you with the love
God has given to you?
Is your cup full and running over?
Do you reach out, share with others,

Or hibernate?
My prayer is that more people
Will see Jesus shining through you;
Through me too,
And that it is His perfect will
We gladly do.
If God can move so mightily
Through a little book,
Such as the tract "Freedom Rider"
How much more through a person
With a "Jesus look?"
Is Jesus shining through you,
Or is He in the Bible only?
Ask Him to show you
Who others see.
Who do you reflect?
Are you all aglow?
Is Jesus someone
You really *know*?

This is what life is all about, this is what makes life worth living that personal relationship with Jesus Christ. He took me out of hell and now I could see how He could use even me and the more He did the more I wanted Him to so do.

RAINBOW RIDER

I did experience something that really gave me a scare on the bike once. As we were driving along, suddenly the driver quickly ducked straight down so low that all I could see was the highway through the windshield. He then straightened up and said: "Now you know what it feels like to be in the driver's seat." I quickly said, "Just stay where you are."

The thought of me ever driving a bike was rejected very quickly. I was praying God would give me the right Christian man for me, and I could be a passenger on his bike. No gears for me to change and fiddle with, or stalling the bike, and whatever else drivers fret about. I just wanted to get married and we could spread the gospel together.

When I returned home from the Niagara Falls' Son Rally, I learned that the couple who gave me a ride in their car were selling their bike the next spring. His wife asked me if I was interested in driving a bike. My heart dropped to my stomach when she said this, and I quickly informed her that I had no desire to drive at all.

Much as I loved biking, driving was not part of my plan. But, when I learned their bike was only 400 c.c.'s and in immaculate condition, I must admit I felt like a fish that had just bit onto a hook, and even though I was by no means reeled in, I was on the hook. Not only that, I had all winter to think about the possibility of owning my own bike, and learning to drive.

Then one of the girls from I.C.B.A. told me that she had taken a course at the College and recommended this to anyone who wanted to learn to drive a motorcycle. She was very adamant about it and told how what she had learned saved her life on a recent trip to the U.S.A.

It sure seemed to me that the Lord was knocking on my door, and I couldn't seem to get away from that knock. Clear as it was though, I cringed at the very thought of driving a bike, all by myself. I do drive a car, but this is a whole new ball game and I knew it. Nevertheless, I did make an agreement with the owner of the 400 cc that he would give me first bid on the bike in the spring. They said they would pray about this.

I really thought it would be easier for God to give me a husband, but He had not done so, and the prospects weren't very enlightening because I wasn't even dating anyone, so I began to think more seriously about driving…with only two wheels under me. Whew…

Meanwhile, as happy memories increased over the summer, I did my best to write a poem that would capture some of my thoughts and vision while riding.

4

Surrounded By A Rainbow

How a person could ever describe
The beauty and majesty I have seen this summer
While riding a motorcycle
For the first time
Is beyond me
The colorful rolling hills
Keep flashing by
Some fields are covered
With bales of hay
Tractors, wagons and laborers

RAINBOW RIDER

Toiling each day
Corn is growing taller and taller
Stretching up to the billowy clouds
In the sky
While the warm sun shines down
On everyone.
It makes me want to cry
The beauty of it all
As I recognize the Master's touch
The more I see, the more I realize
That Jesus loves us very, very much
He has revealed himself to me
So many times
As I've been rolling down the highway
The colors keep increasing,
Yet continue to contrast & blend
Regardless the time of day
Flowers blossom and bloom
From the fields, the planters,
Window boxes, gardens, trees
They are appreciated
As is the warm breeze
It's almost like being surrounded
By a rainbow

Beauty envelops me from north, south,
East & west
No matter where I go
Soaring like an eagle
Is not hard to do
When you keep seeing Jesus
All around you
I'm so glad my spiritual eyes are open
To recognize Him
Yet this poem describes but a pinch
Of what my eyes have seen
In the brief time I've been a passenger
On a motorcycle
What about you…have you seen Jesus
In the places where you've been
You know you can't
Get away from Him
No matter how fast your bike will go
So I pray you slow down And let Him direct your life
As into the world and
Down the holy highway you go
You will have a melody in your heart
Love like an ocean
Joy like a fountain, peace like a river
Every day
Especially when your purpose

RAINBOW RIDER

Is to Uplift Jesus Christ
And win souls
As you ride for the Son
With I.C.B.A.

5

Knock, Knock, Knock

Did you ever hear a knock at the door and without looking to see who was there, you just *knew?* I feel like that right now as I wait for someone special to knock at my door and *I know that I know… who!*

When you have the call of God on your life, there is just no way you can get away from that call, and ever be happy, regardless of how hard you try or how successful you are at running in the opposite direction. You just cannot out run God. I don't care how fast you are, He will always be faster and do a better job too; that's why He knows best how to slow you down and get the response He wants from you. I know, because He sure slowed me down and knew how to break this vessel so He could then pour through…as well as answer a prayer I've prayed for several years.

From August through May God had been gently and lovingly nudging me about learning to drive a motorcycle. There was no way I could get away from this call and I knew it, so finally I phoned the College in Peterboro, Ontario, Canada that offered the training course and they mailed the registration form to me. That fact that I had the money to take the course ($129.00) was one way I knew God was in it, because it had been quite a while since I'd had that much cash on hand.

Perhaps this is a good time to inject a bit about how God's ways are higher. I was gloriously saved on October 22, 1978 at which time I was a divorced single parent, working full time in an office. For one year I worked, then my contract was not renewed and I was at home collecting unemployment insurance while looking frantically for employment. I put my name in many places and was confident that I would get a good job because I had updated my skills, had almost ten years office experience, typed 85 wpm, and wanted to work. But I was not called one time about a job interview in over four months. Finally, I gave up trying. I told the Lord that I was willing, but if the door wasn't open, what else could I do?

In the meantime, I began to develop further the writing talent he had given me, plus I wrote many new songs and poems. My time was not wasted watching soap operas on television, it was spent studying the Word of God, or writing and being as creative as I could be. God honored my obedience. He gave me a complete peace about being home. A single parent is needed at home. God would supply my needs because I had put my trust in Him. I would check the ads and make some calls, but every single time it fell though. I would fill out an application form, mail my resume, and only once in all that time did I get called for an interview.

I came second, and it was at that time that God revealed to me that I had not been writing and spending the time as He had led me to. So, if I would not fulfill this call on my life, then He would use me elsewhere…behind a desk in an office…etc. It was a 'wow' moment. His viewpoint is huge. So I repented, became more disciplined and produced much more, as He was faithful to inspire me to write. I wrote my first book; the manuscript was all typed and ready for publication and it would be done at a time when God would receive the most glory for it. But, in the meanwhile, I was still home, writing for hours at a time and loving it.

It was so easy for people to ask me if I was working... (to them I was not) but they did not see the hours of work I did and the reams of paper that had filled dresser drawers as I continued to produce. They were looking at circumstances and seemed to assume that if a person was a single parent she must be employed. Well, a single parent has a very important job being a mother and I learned this is a full-time job alone, not to mention all the writing I was doing. That's why I soon learned that people would not understand, so I might as well just press a little closer to Jesus and trust Him to bless me in whatever way He chose to as He is my spiritual husband. He would not let me down. I found out He has a reward system. A good one.

What did he do? **He had a lady take me on a shopping spree one day and I came home with $450.00 worth of new clothes. Several people invited my daughter and I to dinner, plus a friend arrived with several bags of frozen meats from her freezer for**

us. I was given an electric typewriter that enabled me to keep up with my writing, and an office chair, and my dad built me a desk, a left-handed desk, so to speak. ☺ There were many more ways in which God met needs, but the important thing I learned was that God does meet your needs when you put Him first, and when you need a miracle...you will have one!

I learned to live with a bank account balance of about $3.00-$5.00 (you can check that decimal point because it is correct, it is *not* a typographical error) for two weeks at a time. Often, I had only change in my purse, no bills, *But*...my bills were paid and I got by. The more I lived like this, the more I got to know Jesus in a personal way and learned how faithful He is. My faith was growing and fear lessened.

You may say, "Yah, but you have to work to make a living...". I was working as I learned to walk by faith and you cannot please God without faith. Now I needed faith to follow the instructions as I drove on the college parking lot to begin lessons. I put the dirt bike in gear. About 19 other students did the same. The adrenalin was flowing and was about to increase.

6

Up, Up And Away

With 125 cc's under me, a heart that was relatively calm under the circumstances, as a young man behind my bike was about to give it a good push. I aimed the bike for the instructor! Well, not really... well... yes, I did, but let me explain. He told us to look up... look at him; not at the yellow line we were supposed to stop the bike on! So, I did, and I found out it works pretty good because before long I had stopped the bike on the line three times and was able to move on to the next lesson.

(For the non-drivers, the front brake lever is located above the right handlebar, and the rear brake control is located to the front of the right footrest. They should be used simultaneously…unless you want to get thrown over the handlebars, and wet roads call for greater caution.

There are many details to cover, but since this book is *not* a motorcycle training course, I'll share only what I feel is pertinent testimony. I started the bike and surprised myself by stopping safely the first time, even though first gear was as high as we had gone thus far. Some of the students advanced to second gear but I did not feel confident enough yet, so I continued in first for a few more short runs. It was during one of these runs that I got the surprise of my life!

When you drive a bike, your right wrist should be in a limp position when you start. *Mine wasn't!* Consequently, when the speed increased it did so quickly, not gradually, and the engine noise whined shrilly, much to my alarm. My head was telling my hand and feet to brake, but the speed was increasing and as I heard the engine rev further, I recall thinking: **"That's *my* bike!"** I recalled the instructor saying that if we had a problem, not to try to save the bike, so what did I do? **I let go of everything…including the clutch!** *Dumb move!*

The next thing I knew I was headed for heaven as the front wheel lifted off the ground. I flew by, looked down to see the instructor looking up at what was going on and *noticed that his mouth dropped open.* As the bike and I parted company I hoped it would not fall on me because I was obviously going to land before it did…even though it weighs more. I watched the smooth black pavement looming toward me as I plunged through the air. At this moment, I took a deep breath and said one word only: **"Lord!"** I remember thinking, **"This is going to HURT!"**

For a flash of a second I wondered if this would be a case of "Sudden death, sudden glory!" Not so. The *touchdown* was followed by immediate and acute pain. (Surely Humpty Dumpty felt like this when he fell off the wall.) I rolled over on my back right away, looked up and saw the blue sky, the sunshine, bikers and bikes not far away, as I was in their pathway so I hoped they would not run over me. (No offense intended, bikers.)

Then I realized I had stopped breathing. I tried to take a breath and couldn't. I then became aware that as I lay on my back my shoulders and head were resting on someone's knees as that person knelt behind me. It was the instructor I had seen just seconds before with his mouth open as he watched me learn to fly. He didn't say a word; he was quiet, but he was there, and that was a comforting help.

I probably should mention that when the front wheel reared in the air and I was heaven bound, all I could think of was just because Rainbow Rider is my name, does not mean I plan to drive that high and ride the rainbows…literally! *Rainbow Rider was the name I thought of one day because it just clicked together since Rainbow had been my name for ten years when I used a citizen's band radio.*

As I lay on my back I remembered something the Lord showed me a long time ago. It seemed so appropriate right now. He said, "Together We will ride the rainbows and together We will push the plow." Somehow, the suffering I had just plunged into showed me we were now pushing the plow, but I knew We would ride the rainbow yet… even though I heard voices from a distance saying, "How is her leg? Is she okay? How is her leg? I did not hear the instructor answer, but I recall thinking: **"Never mind my leg…I need some air! I can't breathe!"** But they didn't know that, and as I tried again to inhale…, unsuccessfully; I started to see blackness and I thought if I could lay flat I would not faint.

Once again, I called upon the Lord, saying, **"Lord, help me, I don't want to faint. Help me please Lord."** I struggled to move my shoulders and head aside and the instructor realized I wanted to lay flat so he then helped me. Believe it or not, as he lowered my head to the pavement I was trying to lower it straight down *so as not to scratch my helmet...* I wonder if any guys in my position would have thought of that? Once a woman, always a woman! Praise the Lord!

Well I did not actually pass out, I remained conscious, which means I was fully conscious of the pain also. My lungs felt like they had just gone through a wringer washer, my ribs hurt so badly I could feel all forty-two of them, at least it felt like there were that many. My left knee was just screaming as the pain shot down my leg and up my leg until I didn't know what hurt the most. I felt like a grenade that had just exploded so I didn't quite know how to go about picking up the pieces as I attempted to get it together.

As I glanced to my right, dear old faithful was lying there too, and both wheels were as still as could be. She looked okay, but I must admit I was glad it wasn't my bike, *I even thought that when I was about to depart from the bike as we were headed straight up!* Bad enough to have an accident, but to put my ripples in my own bike would be much more upsetting... at least I was able to be thankful for something... chuckle!

I attempted to get up, then realized I better lay back a bit longer because my head was swirling and the parking lot appeared to be on a real tilt. It didn't take long for me to bend that leg and see that it was movable. Since the pain was so severe I prayed that nothing would be broken. I didn't care how bruised I was as long as I could continue. This course was so important to me and I was determined not to let anything rob me of achieving this goal.

I got up, checked all my parts and was confident that nothing was broken, not to mention very, very relieved. I declined the offer to go to the hospital, but pointed out that if I really thought something was broken, I would go. I also promised to see my family doctor when I got home. **The instructor taped the brake lever together for the time being, and did a complete safety check of the bike as I took a breather.** He didn't know it, but I was saying, ***"Thank-you Lord, that I am okay, I really don't think anything is broken, and that is a miracle. Thank you for protecting me.***

I do have some questions… but we will have to talk later. Right now, I must get on that bike!"

Once again, I raised my right leg over the rear wheel and seat and positioned myself on the bike. As my hands gripped the handlebars, I took a breath and realized that something had just gripped me… *fear*! I looked at the instructor and said: *"This is the hardest part… isn't it… getting back on… after an accident?"* He looked at me with a serious face, then a hint of a grin escaped as his eyes showed compassion and he nodded yes. I was glad he was honest about it and did not try to be flippant. There is a time to be serious and a time for frivolousness.

I am frank, so I must tell you this too. When I looked up at this time, I said, "Lord, protect me." But inside I was hurting because it seemed like the Lord had let me down…and *hard*. I knew it was only by the grace of God that I had no broken bones. But I also knew how much I hurt, and I had prayed for protection before, so it was hard to have faith in that protection. However, my desire to drive a bike was stronger than the fear, so I increased the throttle and released the clutch… slowly… to be sure… and moved the bike out of the way. So far, so good. (Whew.)

One of the instructors said at the beginning of the course, **"If you're not nervous…you *should* be."** Well he didn't have to worry now, because I *was nervous!* I could hardly believe all of this had happened and I hadn't even put that bike in second gear yet! Talk about humbling… embarrassing… humiliating… you name it, but somehow, I didn't really care about all that. All I could see was a goal and I was not about to quit. Quitting didn't even cross my mind. All I knew was to go for it and not doubt. I was determined to do it.

The other students were shaping up pretty well by then. At least it looked pretty good to me. They were in second gear and following one another in a circle as they began to use hand signals. Then they advanced to a figure eight.

I stood beside my bike and felt like a hockey player that has been benched… ugh! For a moment, my heart sank because as I watched the others I felt like I would never get caught up. This course was moving the students right along and I could easily tell that no one could afford to lose any time. I wondered if I would be able to bend my leg in the morning, not to mention be able to drive a bike. Nevertheless, I observed the students until it was time for all of us to go to the college for a one-hour lecture which was scheduled at the end of each class. At least I wouldn't miss that.

Some of the students touched my heart by the compassion they showed in asking how I was feeling. One of the girls said she was fine until she looked up, saw me go through the air, land on the pavement, then *slide*. She then started to shake. Well I did not know until then that I had slid, so when she said it, I didn't shake, but I felt a little sick to my stomach.

My leather jacket had been worn right off the front at my rib section, and one elbow. Just minutes before the accident the instructor had told us to do up our jackets and I am so grateful. I also learned the importance of wearing leather because my elbow which turned black in a full circle, (I have pictures to prove it.) also had a road burn for about five inches toward my wrist, yet the skin was not broken because I was protected by the leather. It pays to be protected preferably by leather and by prayer!

Well I tried to pay close attention during the lecture, but I think I was in shock because I just couldn't concentrate. And I was so tired I could hardly stand up. Talk about feeling like you've been pulled through a knothole…! I went limping down the stairs and could only hope and pray that I would be able to return the next day and participate.

That evening I think I woke up every hour and bent my leg to be sure I could do so. I wanted to continue so badly. The heating pad helped, but I hurt so many places that I had to keep moving the heating pad around. Guess I needed an electric blanket to do the job effectively. Anyway, I got up in the morning, put my blue jeans on and was glad to be alive. I put a tensor bandage around my knee to give it some support and we headed for the college. When we arrived I had to take the bandage off, the pain was so bad.

The students arrived and one of the girls informed me that she had brought a special bandage for my knee if I wanted to borrow it. She had therapy on her knee and had been using it. To me she was like an angel because this bandage enabled me to be able to participate the second day. It exposed the kneecap but supported the rest of the knee, so there was no pain and I was sure relieved. Another green light and I knew God was looking after me. *Well I thought He was, but day two proved to be more challenging than I had expected, in more ways than one!*

7

One Potato, Two Potato, Bam!

WITH A DETERMINATION to keep my bike upright and to stay on top of it, I waited for the class to arrive. Since I was still feeling quite concerned about catching up with the rest of the class, I talked to one of the instructors and told him I did not have the confidence to join in with the rest yet, and wondered if I could try a few figure eight's and signals on my own before they started. He walked me to the parking lot where the bikes were parked. Would you believe only three bikes were there and one of those three was the only white bike that I was using! Praise the Lord. He looks after every detail! It felt like a Hi-Five from God.

While I practiced the other bikers were driven to the barn to get their bikes, then drove them to the lot I was using. This gave me about ten minutes before they were actually lined up and ready to go. That was all I needed to increase my confidence and get me rolling. From then on, we worked together like a team. But I think I had to work harder than the rest because every move triggered pain and made it hard to concentrate. I felt "outstanding in a crowd" as the bikes lined up and moved forward, because I knew the big bandage that was wrapped around my left knee must have stood out like a sore thumb…sore knee! I couldn't help it though, and tried not to let it bother me. I certainly didn't want to draw any attention to me. The previous day's crash was center shot enough to last me for a lifetime! Pride is ugly, eh?

Four hours of practice means four hours of steady concentration plus the physical exertion and I knew I was not the only one that was exhausted after class. Mentally I wasn't sure how I would remember everything. I had not yet opened the book on biking that we were given on the first day, and things were progressing so quickly on this second day of training, that I didn't think I'd feel too perky when we finished. We had covered balancing and braking, cold starting, clutch operation and control synchronization, correct gear changing, signals and shoulder checks, pattern riding and slow riding.

Not too shabby for eight hours on the road. Like I said, there was no wasted time in this course. For lack of a better word I call it a *crash course!* (No offense fellows, the accident was not any fault of yours and I know it, so hang loose.)

Picture the bikers spread out on the parking lot as pylons indicated where we were to stop, turn, etc. The noise of the bikes caused the adrenaline to flow and make me feel like they were getting somewhere… even if many were not sure where they were going. At one point, I got the bike in third gear, geared down, came to a full stop. Then I made a sharp right turn from pavement onto a gravel pot holed area upon which I had to make a sharp U-turn around one ugly pylon, then come to a full stop next to the instructor. Well that may sound very basic and easy. Not so!

I managed to gear down... full stop... right turn slowly over the potholes. When I surprised myself by actually getting around the point in the U-turn, I looked up at the instructor for a split second (probably for praise because of making that last corner successfully). *But... as I looked at him I forgot that where you look... is where you go.* Consequently, like in the beginning I found myself headed directly for the instructor! Not good.

Increasing the throttle briefly when one tire dove into a large pothole didn't help matters either. He darted to the right, then changed his mind and darted to his left, while simultaneously positioning himself behind a steel post. I really did look at the next pylon when I realized my mistake and tried my hardest to get that bike pointed at twelve o'clock... rather than two... as I approached the full stop, but it was too late. My intentions were good, but there would be a price to pay for that distraction. The front wheel missed the instructor (by a hair) but the right handle bar did not miss the steel post. Since my fingers were gripped tightly on the front brake lever, my knuckles were bouncing off the steel post one by one until I decided to part company with the lever because the steel post just wouldn't bend.

At least I kept the foot brake for the rear wheel pressed down and stopped the bike. This part hurts, but I must be honest, so I have to confess: I dropped the bike at this point. ☹

The ground to the right of the intersection was a mound of grass that just did not like that front tire sliding over it and that is exactly what happened, the bike slid. So did I while trying frantically to protect my left knee because I knew if I landed on it, I would faint for sure. At least I moved a lot more quickly this time, than I did the first time I dropped the bike. Mind you, the other bikes were at that intersection and I really didn't have any confidence that they would do any better than I did. Plus, I certainly did not want to get run over by one of them.

I waved my hands to signal them to stop because my knee just would not move quickly and the pain was…what can I say? (I was glad this was Sunday and we would have the week to recuperate before starting the following Saturday!)

In the lecture, we were told the length of time it takes before the impact when there is a bike accident.

It is all of two seconds. When I looked at the instructor as I came around the corner, instead of looking at the pylon where I wanted to go, that was the beginning of 'One Potato…Two Potato' as the front wheel went wide and off track.

"Bam"… was when the steel post and I made contact. This is why defensive driving is so important and proves there is little margin for error. I learned the hard way, but you can be certain of one thing: *I learned!*

The instructor helped me up, got the bike upright, filled out an accident report, while **I slowly pulled my leather glove off my right hand and held my breath as I looked at that third finger that had rebelled against the steel post the strongest. It was swelling quickly and discolored… much as I told myself it was not turning blue, it was; in a full circle half way down just below the joint.**

I kept looking at it and slowly tried to bend every joint. Much as it hurt, I could do so and that was all I needed to know. I said silently, *"Lord, I have to drive and can't if this is broken. In the Name of Jesus, please heal this finger so I can continue. I will not let anything stop me, and Jesus paid the price for me to be healed, so I thank you for doing so, in Jesus' Name."*

My finger did not feel any different, but I've learned to walk by faith, not by feelings, so I put my glove back on and mounted the bike. All I wanted to do was get out of there and get going! I did not realize that someone had been watching me and that particular instructor was now at my side.

He looked at me and said, **"You're not getting back on that bike!!"** My heart sank momentarily because I thought he wasn't going to let me continue... (maybe they were worried about the bike getting totaled!).

I looked directly at him as I straddled that bike and said, **"Yes... it's okay... nothing's broken!"**

He paused, seemed speechless for a moment as he looked at me with his heart hanging out and then said, **"I admire your stamina Babe, but what about your leg?!!"**

Once again I looked directly at him and said without hesitation: **"I'm not a quitter... I'm a Christian!"**

The words were a solid hit as he stepped back instantly and with both hands open and raised upward to signify release, he simply said, **"Okay, okay."** And I took off across the parking lot with a big smile from deep within. Once again God had been faithful to give me the words I needed, not to mention tenacity.

The balance of the four hours proved very challenging because I had trouble making a sharp turn at the foot of a hill; then coming to a full stop at the top of the hill. Often there was a lineup of stopped bikes as they climbed the hill and it was not uncommon to see a stalled bike on the hill. Consequently, I had lots of practice in learning how to handle this kind of a situation. It was not... my favorite part of the course.

To kick-start you have to take your right foot off the rear brake, so this means you better not release the front brake or you'll find reverse fast. Also, if you doodle around with the clutch trying to find the friction point, the bike will roll back. So it was a situation that called for concentration and good coordination, not to mention intestinal fortitude as you did your best to become a specialist. You learned **you must control the bike, not let the bike control you!**

RAINBOW RIDER

It is at times like this one needs to have a strong determination to win. I felt like this course would either make or break me and now that it is over, I know I was right. It broke me because I needed to realize the bike was like a bucking bronco that wanted to throw me at the first chance. And as I sat on that bronco, I had to know how to break his spirit or he would get me. After the beating I took, I found my determination to succeed increased and this is when I really won. Because I got a vision of that bike as the kind of weapon it *could* become if I did not control *it. The instructor was right.* Consequently, I then felt much more confidant because I had things in the right perspective. Fear of God and fear of the bike.

I knew the bike and I would become a team that worked together, never separately again! We had to be like a hand inside a glove, so close to each other there was no margin for error. It was no longer the bike and I, it was 'WE'. *Kind of like it is when a person lets Jesus live His life through that individual. Jesus is on the interior and cannot be seen, but He is the power source that motivates all the action, and there never is any failure or short- circuiting when He is the power source.*

8

Lookin' Good

AFTER FIVE DAYS of rest and recuperation I enjoyed the bike ride with my brother from Bowmanville, Ontario to Lakefield, Ontario. The third day of training was drawing nigh. That doesn't mean my aches and pains were gone, they weren't. The bruises had turned a deep purple, but as the doctor stated, nothing was broken. I must admit I enjoyed telling the doctor I had a *five-point checklist*. Then I proceeded to reveal the bruises, arm, ribs, stomach, elbow, and one knee. The doctor said, **"You could have been killed!"**

When I saw a second doctor after x-rays were taken, and told him I was taking lessons when this happened, he said, **"I hope you improve!"** Somehow, I felt he was referring to my driving, not my physical condition.

Something else that has just come to mind is the fact that God inspired me to take a big breath just prior to "touchdown" and this acted as a cushion to protect me when I landed. Immediately following the impact, I rolled over and you know what happened after that, but I feel it is vital to point this out. God did not let me down. He did protect me. Just because you run into problems and difficulties does not mean that God is not in it.

You can be sure you are in a spiritual battle and the devil does not want you to do anything that will be effective in winning souls. That's why I'm so glad for the promise in 1John 4:4 "Greater is He that is in me than he that is in the world." The devil has been defeated and as long as I remain in submission to God I know I'll come through victorious, even though at times it will seem like I am walking in the dark, I know I am not because Jesus is alive in me. There are times when He leads me into areas of danger, but He will be there with me, and will bring me out of those areas too, so why worry. Like a song that I wrote says, *"Why should I worry, why should I fret, my God has never ever failed me yet. He never changes, He's still the same, Jesus Christ is His Name."* It's true too!

I knew He was with me on this third day, the same as He was on the first two days, so I joined the rest of the class and we covered more ground. I hesitated to tell you some of the things we were doing by now because I do not want to deter any of you from taking this course. The important thing to remember is that we were taught what we needed to know in order to help us drive well. So this meant we needed to know what to do if we ever had to avoid an obstacle in the road.

Consequently, there was a section where we had to negotiate collision avoidance. This means a green light was turned on signifying we would make a sharp left, or a sharp right in order to avoid the pylons that had been strategically placed. We had to get the bike in second gear, then release the throttle, and not brake as we received the signal directing our turn.

RAINBOW RIDER

Easier said than done, but it *is* possible! Practice makes perfect...need I say more?

The pylons were put in place and we had the opportunity to avoid each one as we did what they called the serpentine. Actually, it was easier than it looked. The secret is in looking where you want to go and doing so with the right timing. I had already learned the importance of that, so it helped me to put it into action now.

Another fun thing was the little wooden ramp we had to drive over while remembering not to look down, rather to chin up and look ahead and before you knew it, you were over the ramp and all was well. The second ramp was a little more challenging because it was like a 'teeter totter'. We drove up one side and as the front tire passed the center of the board, the other half proceeded to dip down and as I stood with my feet on the pegs I learned to lean forward with the bike when it proceeded to do a nosedive.

Also, I learned not to approach the platform too slowly or it became more difficult. A bit of practice and this challenge was met, so I was on to the next.

The pylons had been moved to form a figure eight around which we were to take the bike while simultaneously keeping the bike within three feet of the circle. Again, it took control, concentration, and was not as bad as it appeared at first. By now a lot of what we had done became easier because of the practice, but I was at a disadvantage in not having a bike at home that I could practice on. I learned that a lot of the students already had bikes. So it didn't take me long to stop comparing my skills with theirs (or lack of skills) because there was no comparison. I had never even driven a car with a clutch. Consequently, since I really was a greenhorn at biking, I knew that if I could pass this course, *anyone* could...with God's help. And fortitude.

The entire four hours passed and I had not dropped the bike even once. You can smile. It was just great to feel so much better about learning to drive, and I must commend the instructors who seemed to know just when to offer praise and encouragement, and when to yell an exhortation, and when to be still. They really do not have an easy job and the more I learned, the more I learned to appreciate some of the difficulties they had as instructors. For sure they needed lots of patience, not to mention courage. I'm not so sure I would want to be out there watching all those bikes coming at me when I knew the drivers were not necessarily going to stop just because the pylons indicated a stop.

This, plus the fact that at least we felt a breeze as we were driving, but they had to stand in the hot sun and watch us for four hours at a time. They had to move around, yes, but they were out there in the hot sun, and in the rain as well. For this, I say, *"Thank you fellows; for your dedication because without your dedication and persistence I would not be out there today. Keep your wheels right side up and take care."*

The third day finished and I left feeling very encouraged, satisfied, not overly confident. *My bike and I had become friends rather than fighters* and for this I was glad. I passed the written test and was even looking forward to the fourth day of teaching, but I wasn't looking forward to the road test following the teaching.

9

Eleventh Hour

When the fourth day arrived I was thankful that we had had perfect sunny weather for the entire four days. I hopped on the 125 c.c.'s and headed for the parking lot, along with the rest. We followed one another around the course and I was feeling happy because of a quick move I made that avoided a collision, prior to the testing.

During the course, we have to jump a curb at one point, drive over the grass and down over the other curb, then across the parking lot. The biker ahead of me dropped his bike just after jumping the curb. I kept enough cushion around the bike that as I looked ahead and saw this happen, I took an alternate route and was able to continue on without incident. The teaching from the slides during one of the lectures was proving beneficial.

A second time I approached the same curb while the biker ahead of me stalled his bike just after jumping the curb. Since the bike remained upright I swerved just a bit to the right and jumped the curb. But… in those few seconds he dropped his bike and there was not enough room for his wheels to slide to the right *without avoiding my front wheel, which his rear wheel slid into!* **(Can you believe it?)**

This resulted in my wheels being knocked right out from under me. The next thing I knew I was standing on the grass feeling like a fool. It upset me to have this happen when I had been doing to much better, and I learned that I *could* pick up a 125 c.c.'s. Especially when I am upset! **I took time to pluck the grass and sod off the clutch pedal; after all, we were about to have our test and I didn't want this kind of evidence to influence the examiner in any adverse way.** I needed all the help I could get so I wasn't taking any chances on even one blade of grass causing a negative thought. I brushed my knee off too and hopped on again, once I felt we were as roadworthy as we could be, under the circumstances. I must admit it seemed like it was a lot later than it was as far as time was concerned, but it wasn't. I couldn't believe that spill would unnerve me so much. *I tried to compose myself, but I felt shaky from then on.*

I began to have problems stalling the bike and that had not been a problem before. This caused further alarm as the eleventh hour was fast approaching, but what could I do? The instructor called all of us off the bikes and somewhat gently raked us over the coals verbally...for looking so sloppy out there. He told us that if we didn't smarten up we would not pass our test. We were told the areas where we needed to improve and sent back to try again. (Ugh! As if I didn't know I was in trouble... oh well... he was just doing his job... I guess what made me mad is the fact that I knew he was right.)

We had a bit of time to practice further, then the lessons were over and it was nitty gritty time. The test was in three sections. You had to pass the first two before you could enter the third, the road test. Well I made it to the road test, but I did not have an assurance that all was well. To be honest, I felt like everything was quite rushed.

RAINBOW RIDER

Mind you, I missed about an hour of teaching that first day, plus the pain that hindered my driving, it seemed an impossible situation. However, I was determined to do my best, and that is all anyone could do. It was not until this moment though, as the students gathered together waiting for their name to be called, that I realized I had missed an important part of the road signals and shoulder checks. There was confusion as I listened to them and I knew I was in trouble.

This part of the test was not something I looked forward to at all. I felt like someone who was about to have a math test and knew how to add, subtract and multiply, but had just learned there would be division on the test too! So, it was hard to think positively, let alone concentrate, and it is important to have a good mental attitude.

My name was called. I was on deck. With my bike in position, I sat there saying silently, "God, I need a miracle…" (as if He didn't know. Ha!). Then they motioned me forward. I looked up and did exactly what no one ever wants to do…**I stalled the bike, right then and there in front of all the students, spectators, the whole shebang.** (Oh well, I won't let that get to me, I'll just try again and it will be okay.)

Any bets? I concentrated, increased the throttle, began to release the clutch and did a perfect repeat performance!! ☹ **My ears heard laughter from the spectators, even through my helmet.** *(Incidentally, in case you were a spectator with a video camera I sure would love a copy of the road test, believe it or not.)* Fortunately, I did not hear any from the students in our class or I may have forgotten I am a Christian and took pursuit. *If there had been a pinhole in the ground I would have gladly slid through, but there wasn't.* I could hardly believe my ears when that bike stalled a second time. I could almost feel the class pulling for me as they stood by quietly.

Surely, I don't have to tell you how fast my heart was beating as I sat there and suddenly it was very, *very, very, hot under that helmet.* I didn't dare look at the two instructors in the half ton truck that were about to follow me because if I did... and they were laughing *I really think I would have gotten off that bike and lambasted one of them.* Nasty, yes, but I also know that if I had been in their place it would have been hard not to laugh. Gee... and all I wanted to do was get my "M" license. If anyone had ever told me there would be days like this I never would have believed it.

Suddenly, I heard a horn followed by a voice as one instructor called my name. I looked to my left almost defying him to say anything at all. He said, **"That doesn't count, you know. Your test doesn't start until you get on the road. You're still in the parking lot."** I nodded. (Embarrassing or what... *Lord, what is this, humble Linda day? It's not like I am trying to do this myself. I already asked for Your help, you know that...!*) The instructor then said, **"Take a deep breath, Relax."** *(Easy for him to say. If I ever get through this, I'm not so sure I'll want... to do it again!)*

I did get through it though, the third attempt proved successful and I finally completed the course. Even though I held my right arm out to make a right turn... yep. Sure did. Wanted to be sure those behind me knew that I knew... where I was going. When I parked the bike, it was almost a relief to get off it, and I felt like I was in shock. From first thing this morning things had gone wrong, yet yesterday was so great.

I sat down and said, *"Thanks Lord, for helping me get this far, but to be honest, I don't think I passed. Sorry I didn't do better, but I did do my best. I just need more time. I'm glad You do not condemn me Lord. If I am wrong and I did pass the test, don't let me be deceived. Please send someone over to encourage me."*

I waited while looking at that black pavement. I heard footsteps coming my way, but they passed me. This happened *five* times and not one word was said to me. *"It's okay Lord. I get the message. I just didn't make it. I know you called me to do this, so I don't understand why I didn't pass. Please prepare me concerning this disappointment Lord, because I don't want to cry when that instructor tells me I didn't pass. Thanks for the peace you've given me, in the midst of it all. I give my disappointment to you Lord, and ask for strength and help. Take the pain out of this knee and these ribs too, while you're at it. Help me now to face the others and to be an encouragement to them, in Jesus' Name. Amen."*

I felt two tears fall, gently wiped them away with a hanky I had in my leather jacket, then stood up and observed the others. Out of seventeen entrants (one had dropped out and a second had hurt her hand so would return later) I was finished the testing quite early. Since there was nothing to do but wait, I decided to go back to the second section of testing and see how the others were doing.

One of the girls had just completed the second section of testing and was very upset. For the first time in the four-day period, she dropped her bike this morning and was devastated. I knew how she felt because of getting my wheels knocked out from under me at the curb. Her language was very crude, but I knew she was hurting and tried to be compassionate. I told her that I am a Christian and the only way I can go out there is to ask God to help me.

She listened while I told her to get hold of her emotions and chin up. She had done very well and it was easy to see she was very stable with the bike, at least in comparison with me, (doesn't say much for her... does it?) but she wouldn't succeed the third section if she didn't regain composure. I put my arm around her as we talked and silently asked God to help her. I really wanted her to pass. Even though most of the students did not know each other, we were comrades pulling for each other to do well. They pulled and I prayed. Guess what happened... *she passed and I didn't! Figure that out...*

For a moment, I had to lift that to the Lord because here I was serving the Lord, trying to live my life as I would if I could *see Jesus*, and there had been many changes, yet this young foul-mouthed student goes out there and gets her license. It didn't seem fair. I never worked so hard at anything over a four-day period as I did this course and it was a big disappointment to me, to say the least.

The fact that I was not the only student to fail really did not make me feel any better. I wanted to win and there were no two ways about it. I knew God loved both this student and I, but I guess it is easy to expect things to be easier when you know the Lord is on your side. God didn't say it would be easier. ***Even a bed of roses has thorns…***

The good thing was that I knew I had done my best and that was all that anyone could do, so I did not criticize myself for failing. When I was told I would have one more chance to try the test in two weeks time, I really wasn't excited about it at all because my desire to drive died… when I got off the bike after the test. It just got up and went! Like I said, I worked very hard mentally and physically, and I wasn't so sure I could go through all that again. I just wanted to sleep and sleep and get rid of all the pain everywhere, interior and exterior. This was good though, because the seed, my vision, had to die before it come to fruition, bring forth fruit. Now the desire to drive could actually be manifested. All I needed was some time to rest and let God minister life to me as only He can do. Restoration was part of the process.

I really felt more stunned than disappointed because it was hard to believe that I really did not pass. It was too bad because the instructors had worked so hard too and I knew that this made it look bad for their record, so that bothered me. I didn't want to be any such statistic. I wanted to be part of their 85% success statistics! After all, this program has gained worldwide recognition as the finest rider-training program anywhere in the world. I think that is what we were told. **Don't stop reading because I failed the test, surely you are not a quitter…? You are just getting to the interesting part where some romance enters the program…** that is, unless I decide to tell you about the fifth DAY before I tell you about the Fifth Amendment. Intriguing…? Read on☺

10

The 5th Amendment

Here it is, the moment you have been waiting for, something juicy and unexpected as I share something unexpected that happened to me. After our training in the parking lot for four hours on the second day, we returned to the college for a lecture lasting one hour. I was sore, tired, but trying my best to hang in there. Little did I know the surprise that God had waiting for me.

During my lecture, I looked up from the second row where I was seated at a desk and there he was, sitting there in living color, as handsome as anyone could be. All I could think was, "Where have I been,

I never saw him in our class before. I better smarten up!" *I even glanced around to make sure I was in the right class. What a hunk!"*

Now maybe that doesn't sound too Christian to you, but I tell it like it is, and I am being honest. (If you were single that long and not dating anyone, don't you think your heart would do a flip if you met someone worth checking out?) I have been single since I've been saved, seven and a half years ago and when you have almost given up on getting married to the right Christian man for you, it is exciting when a new hope appears.

From what I observed, I was very impressed. He had a beautiful smile and a full beard. Was God 'sparking my plugs' or what? This course began to get somewhat more interesting, and I dare say the bruises didn't hurt quite as much either. The class finished and as I headed for the parking lot where my ride home would be. I had to go slower because of my knee, so they were several feet ahead of me. As I approached their car I looked up and I could hardly believe my eyes. There he was, walking across the parking lot **to his bike! Now I was really doing some thinking. He must already**

have his license, but heard about this course and wants to learn further. This thought (judgment) impressed me, plus I noticed in class that he is NOT wearing a wedding ring. (I know that doesn't mean a lot, but it was a good sign as far as I was concerned.)

Now I was really doing some thinking. Not to mention the fact that that I wasn't the only one to see him cross the parking lot, he saw me too and our eyes met for the first time... and it was for a long time, until finally I lowered my eyes before I tripped over a car! I managed to get in and look back but I couldn't see him from where we were parked, so I sat there feeling like a teenager that just met a heartthrob. *"Lord, I'm not so sure I am ready for this....."* I made a mental note to check out the class on the following Saturday and see if he was there.

Saturday finally arrived and I checked and double-checked, but he was gone... groan! Oh well, I should have known. He probably knows so much about biking; he decided to drop the course. It could be for the best though because I am having enough trouble concentrating without him being nearby.

The fourth day arrived and if you remember what you have read, you know this is the day I just couldn't seem to get it together. When I had just about reached the final straw, I removed my helmet, leather gloves, and left the bike proudly standing in line with the others as the class headed toward the instructor that had called us aside. He proceeded to chastise us and while doing so, all of a sudden, I felt something so beautiful. If you are born-again, you will understand what that means but if not, you won't because you have to be born-again to understand the things of the Spirit of God.

What happened is that I could feel God manifesting His love toward me and my eyes were drawn in another direction, as I looked toward the source of what I was feeling. Instantly, my eyes made contact with none other than this guy that I figured had quit. He was standing there looking so super as the sun shone on his full beard and better still, he was looking right at me… for a long, long time. Once again, it was me that broke the contact because I was so surprised to see him, I didn't want to keel over. Sometimes it is hard to be graceful!

I tried to listen to the instructor and pay attention, but I wanted to look again and make sure this guy was not a mirage. Sure enough, there he was, and once again, he was looking right back at me very intently. It was so deep as our eyes met. The students that stood between us just seemed to vanish as he and I became one in the spirit as only two born-again people can do.

By now, I had observed something else... and he knew it. This handsome student was no student! He was the guy who was marking our road test and wore a red T-shirt and cap like the other instructors. It was then that he was introduced by one of the men, and I didn't know where to look. Boy, can I pick them!! (I surmised that he must have been just sitting in on class that second day, checking to see that things were in order. But I was not about to assume anything else because I did think he was a student. Sure goes to show you cannot judge a book by its cover. In fact, sometimes you can't even believe what you see. (Why can't life just be easy and fun, fun, fun?")

The testing began and I advanced to the second section where he was marking students in the collision avoidance and emergency braking. My heart did a little flip when I saw him there and I prayed because I knew I could not afford to get distracted at all. Not that he did anything to distract me... well he did really, he bothered me by just being there. Even if it was a nice kind of bothering...

The second instructor advised me what to do and I proceeded to get the bike in second gear, then as I advanced I watched intently for one of the green lights to come on so I would know which direction to turn as I did the collision avoidance. It finally happened, the light came on, but it was RED. I felt a check in my spirit, but did not brake quickly because THIS was the collision avoidance test. What was going on? Talk about blowing it! I approached the second instructor and said, "What happened to the green light?" He said, **"Linda, this is the emergency brake test, then the other. You get two chances for each, so go back and try again and remember the emergency braking will be first."** Needless to say, I didn't even dare look over to... you know who!

I circled around and this time I braked quickly, looked at the instructor who was nearby and he looked like he would burst. I knew he wanted to tell me something, but he couldn't. Suddenly I clued in...I forgot the safety check over my shoulder, so I quickly looked back (it must have appeared like slow motion) then directly to heaven and said, *"Lord!"*, then to my left and sure enough there he was, tipping his head back as he laughed aloud and wiggled his finger for me to come to him.

What a day! As if I wasn't having enough trouble... now he was wiggling his finger at me. I stopped the bike about ten feet from him and he said, *"I've got a lot of papers to mark today, you don't want me to have to walk that far. Come over here."* I gulped. If he only knew... I was parked right where I was for a reason, I didn't want to **hit** him! Well, he asked for it, so I proceeded with much caution.

When I got closer, he smiled from ear to ear, and said, "A piece of cake!" I looked and said somewhat frustrated, *"Ya, right, a piece of cake!"* Then I prepared for the next test. (I could hardly believe he called me over just to say that... was he making a pass?) I was hoping! Ha Ha

The final test was soon completed and my name was the first one called when our marks were given out. I headed for the other office and was sent to see *"you know who"*. He sat at a big desk and asked for my driver's license. I wanted to ask if he needed it whether I passed or whether I failed, but figured I better be quiet. It crossed my mind that now he would know how old I am and that hardly seemed fair because I didn't see his driver's license!

Oh well. I also didn't see any photos of a wife or kids on the desk, so that was a relief...just in case he did ask me out. For sure I was not dating him unless he was a Christian, and single. So far, it was only by faith that I believed he was both... and I needed to know more. There was no opportunity though. The only chance we had to talk was when he said something about all the paperwork, and I noticed that the florescent lights overhead were off. I mentioned it to him and he said he forgot; but I could turn them on and he nodded toward the switch by the door.

Innocent little me said, *"Well, I was just thinking about your eyes."* (gulp...did I say *that!*) Again, he said I could turn them on and looked at me. This time I headed for the switch, at which time another worker just outside the door looked up from his desk questioningly and I said: *"I'm just turning his light on."*... (did I really say *that*...I've got to stop putting my foot in my mouth!) As I turned to sit down again I was sure I saw a hint of a smile through his beard, as "you know who… lowered his head a bit further while doing the paperwork. Suffice to say the atmosphere was electric!

Just then, the other instructor picked up on my comment and said to *"you know who"*: "Myself I find I always work better in the dark than in the light… what about you?" My heart was in my mouth as I quickly prayed, *"Lord, don't let him be embarrassed."* He paused, looked up, then back at his paperwork while saying very calmly and impressively: **"No comment!"**

Now that comment revealed a lot to me and he certainly won points with me, but if he had given some answer with a sexual connotation I would have lost all interest in him, regardless of how attracted I was to him. So far, I was very impressed, but this was the end of the course, so what next?

He was tactful when telling me that I did not pass, and I knew it was not easy for him. There are parts of every job that individuals find difficult, but he did a good job and this impressed me. Not everyone shows compassion and is sensitive to the feelings of others, but he was and that is a plus. How could I meet someone that impressed me so much, then just leave. This was almost worse than not meeting anyone at all. I guess that old saying may be true, that true love never runs smoothly. One good thing about failing was that **I did get a second chance**, so I figured this could be a double header yet *if I got my M license and the man! All things are possible. Amen? With God! Only one more Chapter left.*

II

Second Chance

TWO FULL WEEKS passed and I came back for a second chance. Walked toward the group of bikes that had already begun and there he was. (*Lord, you better help me, because this guy is really having quite an effect on me, and I really don't know if he is married or not.*) The fact that meeting him caused me to draw closer to the Lord made me more encouraged to believe that he is single, but I needed more information before I was about to pursue any relationship... maybe he felt the same way as I did, but who knows... only God.

We circled the route for a while as we practiced the road run prior to the test. I stalled the bike every time I got to a certain sharp corner that is on a hill. And wouldn't you know it, he stood at that corner. I would have liked to impress him, but no go. He would tell me where I went wrong and encourage me, then step back. It was very business-like and I respected him for this. After all, he was at work. Much as I wanted to talk to him, I had to commend him for good ethics.

I had more trouble at the same corner and this time when he came over, his right hand rested solidly on my back, causing me to perspire even more. Maybe it didn't bother him, but it did me. And if that wasn't causing my heart to beat fast enough, there was another encounter to follow. This time around, I couldn't get the bike started when I stalled it. I had used the kick-start three times and no go.

Thus far, he had always stood on my left as he helped me, but suddenly as I tried to get my breath after kicking three times to no avail, I heard a voice in my right ear say: **"Hold your leg up!"** For a minute, I thought it was a word of knowledge from the Lord, until I turned and saw *"you know who"* attempting to hit the kick-start on my bike. All I could think of was… *what are you talking about…* and I froze right where I was. Talk about shock treatment! He could have warned me a bit, I didn't even know he was there.

He did get the bike started though, then leaned to my ear and said, **"Now get out of here!"** I smiled from ear to ear because I *knew* I was bothering him as much as he bothered me. It was mutual!

That was our last encounter until we headed for the college to the final lecture. As the class went inside, he was beside me and I asked him for more registration forms. He said he didn't have any, and asked the other instructor who was ahead of us with about ten students, if he had some. He did not, but told me there were some in the car. I looked at "you know who" and he looked directly into my eyes and said without hesitation, "We'll get them… later."

Okay! Then the other instructor looked back and said to me: "They are in the front seat of the car, in the console. You can get them." I knew he meant I had time to do so now, but when I turned and looked at "you know who", he said without hesitation once again: "We'll get them… later." My heart did a flip and I nodded, I couldn't even answer him, all I wanted to do was get in that classroom and sit down before my knees buckled. He did add that the other instructor would be later, but we… would get them… later. Now if it was not perfectly clear that he wanted to talk to me, then I don't know what else he could have done to make it so.

But, the student that had offered to drive me to the bus terminal had to leave before all the students had received their marks. I felt terrible, and decided to go to the other office and let "you know who" know that I had to leave early. I hate to say it, but I chickened out because I didn't want to interrupt him when he was with a student, yet could not keep my ride waiting. I lived over an hour away. So, I left and picked up some of the registration forms on my way past the car.

Oh, I almost forgot to tell you what happened when I finished my ***"Second chance"*** road test. I got off the bike and my feet would hardly stay on the ground I was so high. I wanted to jump and shout and couldn't wipe the smile off my face. My ribs and knee were still very sore, but I was celebrating anyway because deep within **I *knew* that I had reached the goal and would have my "M" license, on none other than Mother's Day, May 11.**

I was on top of the mountain with the Lord as I then sought out others who were about to do their test and encourage them. I felt like *'Motorcycle Momma'* then, because all of the girls were much younger than me. Nevertheless, one is never too old to learn, so I *learned.* I learned some things the hard way and had the battle scars to prove it, but some of the experiences were far less painful.

Now what…I have my "M" license but what about the "man"? I had prayed that if it was God's perfect will for "you know who" and I to have a date that God would give him the courage to ask me for a date. Also, that God would prepare the way and I would go, but if it was not His perfect will, to close the door between us.

What did I do? God prepared the way, brought us together in the hall and he made it clear that he wanted to talk to me, but I stood him up. I could hardly believe I stood him up, but I did. The more I thought about this as I got closer to home, the worse I felt. I do not want to hurt anyone and I felt that I had let him down and disappointed him. I prayed about it and felt God wanted me to send a note of apology, so I did.

On Monday I prayed, "Lord, if you want me to send this then give me the words and if it flows freely I will know it is your will for me to do this." I wrote the note and changed only a few phrases, so I used a second card and put it in the pink envelope. I then walked to the post office and mailed it. I did wonder when he would get the message because I did not know where he worked other than part time at the college. I did think he worked elsewhere though because when he shook hands with me I noticed his hands were calloused and wondered if he was a mechanic. I knew he might not get it until Saturday when classes began again for biking, but could hope he would get it sooner.

I prayed that the note would be a blessing and that he would not be embarrassed in any way. I considered the possibility that he was married and even have a wife as secretary, so chose not to put my return address on the envelop and marked it personal. I had no intention of hurting anyone, only in blessing someone and trying to do God's will. It took holy boldness to send that note and I really expected something beautiful to happen as a result.

It was a few days later when I reread the original note and realized I had made a typographical error.

Basically, I apologized for leaving early, explained that the lady who provided transportation for me had to leave early to attend a bridal shower. I thanked him for his help and shared how getting my "M" license was a highlight in my life.

I let him know I was not about to go barreling down the highway and even stated that a tutor would be a great asset. Then I wrote, **"God any suggestions?"** You guessed it, no response, no phone call. Just the memories of joy, pain, and success, in reaching yet another goal on Mother's Day! Glory to God.

Now you have it, a blow-by-blow account of five days in my life that provided material for a book. Proof that "With God all things are possible." Mark 10:27 I have written several more books over the years, but waited until God's timing to publish. Though it is now decades later and this is probably the least spiritual of all the books, poems, and songs I have written, yet this is a book I'm thankful to share with you. I find it triggers a merry heart every time I read it and that is good medicine.

Also, because of seeds that have been planted as I have shared my personal relationship with Jesus

Christ I pray you too will get to know and love Him. Hell is real and so is heaven. God gave every person in the whole world a free will to accept His only begotten Son, Jesus Christ, as Savior and Lord. It is through the blood Jesus shed on Calvary that you can be saved as you pray sincerely, and only through the blood of Jesus. Only Jesus Saves! If you are not saved you can be by praying this prayer right now because God is with you right where you are, and Jesus is knocking on the door of your heart. Only you can open the door.

Let's pray: "Jesus I ask you to come into my heart right now, forgive all of my sins. I receive you as my Savior and ask you to be the Lord of my life. Take control of every area. I proved I can make a mess of my life, now please teach me how You can have something good come out of it all like you promise in Romans 8:28. I want to serve You Jesus. I close the door to the devil.

Thank you, Jesus that my sins are forgiven and You do not condemn me. Teach me how to live for you and to bring glory to you Jesus, and to produce good fruit in my life. I know I must mature spiritually, daily. Help me Holy Spirit, teach me. I will work out my salvation with fear and trembling, it is a process. I pray this in Jesus' Name. Amen.

If you prayed this prayer sincerely, please send me a note and let me know and I will rejoice with you. I will keep writing books too, that God will use as tools for soul winning. Praise the Lord! Glory to God!!!! **He loves bikers too** ☺

FYI: Have you read my book 'The Rent Is Paid?' Available soon.

www.ingramcontent.com/pod-product-compliance
Lightning Source LLC
Chambersburg PA
CBHW071150090426
42736CB00012B/2292